MURMURATION

Poems by Jim McGowin

Kansas City Spartan Press Missouri

Spartan Press
Kansas City, Missouri
spartanpresskc.com

Copyright (c) Jim McGowin, 2018
First Edition 1 3 5 7 9 10 8 6 4 2
ISBN: 978-1-946642-60-8
LCC#: 2018950274

Design, edits and layout: Jason Ryberg
Cover image: Harry Coin
Title page image and author photo: Jim McGowin
All rights reserved. No part of this publication may be reproduced or transmitted in any form or by any means, electronic or mechanical, including photocopying, recording or by info retrieval system, without prior written permission from the author.

Spartan Press would like to thank Prospero's Books, The Fellowship of N-finite Jest, The Prospero Institute of Disquieted P/o/e/t/i/c/s, Will Leathem, Tom Wayne, Jeanette Powers, j. d. tulloch, Jon Bidwell, Jason Preu, Mark McClane, Tony Hayden and the whole Osage Arts Community.

The author would like to thank the editors of these publications, where some of these poems first appeared:

UCity Review, The Gasconade Review

CONTENTS

Exposed / 1

Marmalade / 3

Lethe / 7

Hoax / 10

The Prescription for Burning (for Greg) / 12

Fingers Haunted by Dead Poets (for Lorca) / 14

I, Ophelia / 16

Little Things I've Only Dreamt About / 19

Antigone / 21

Anteros / 23

When the Morrígan Asked to Be My Muse / 26

Mephistopheles is Ready for His Portrait Now / 28

Sing Us a Song so That so Many Poets Will
  No Longer Need to Commit Suicide / 30

Harmonia in Absentia / 46

Binary Collapse / 48

Symbiotic Monsters / 50

Beating Down Words Like Nails / 53

Shipwrecks / 55

Siege Engine / 57

Psalm / 59

Nice to Meet You / 61

Pirouette / 63

Achlys' Lips, Wet With Mercy / 65

Minotauros / 68

The Colossus Has Always Been Hollow / 70

Daughter of Nix / 72

Liminal Deities / 73

MURMURATION

*The crow wish'd everything was black, the owl,
that everything was white.*

-William Blake, *The Marriage
of Heaven and Hell*

Exposed

We thought of them as feet
but they were actually falling asleep,

And I wished for a sudden ceremony
to wash over my thoughts and
to confiscate them,
further complicating
any trick of backtracking.

You were barefoot and saying hello,
taking any excuse to feel anything,

Including a shot at everlasting life,
or an impossibly interlaced odyssey,
devoid of too much ambition.

Compliance was thrown out of
contact from standing too long
at absurd angles,

The imperfection of your pace
wore tears in persuasion,
unable to pay
for a bruised heel.

The resulting deviation
should have been cautionary,

But I was barefoot,
and wanted you to know
never ever,

And I wanted you to know
invariably,

And I wanted you to know
that I did not care
about the luxury of successful cadence,

Or how much more conspicuous you were
when your shoes were on –

The prowess of your deception
was what I was truly dazzled with,

How uncompromisingly you denied
the fluctuations of your own footprints.

Marmalade

It goes deeply as hoaxed daylight
scratching at the joyride candy,
sparkling bait for a bareknuckle autopsy.
I washed my sleepy wear and said
I'm glad to know you,
you and your hemlock bogeymen—
the so called
darlings of everyday existence...

And didn't I warn you? I lie like a grasshopper.

The dread ballet begins,
the one where you fashion the
enlargements of the lower body
into a throat powered by hounds,
a phrase of global drowsiness
only rivaled by its grunting.

I fainted and immediately stopped being killed.

Horsepower forgeries,
daring questions like:
Did you touch the sickness?
Did it let you bludgeon its heartbeat?
Did its bloodlust result in favorable bribes?

Did you probe its humanlike bullwhips
with degenerate jerking?

Everything was drunk to the eyes,
everything was so immensely bovine,
everything was television cosmology,
and no one had to tell the bottoms of
the wishing wells to be empty,
they just inquired about lost spaces
and changed their personalities
to suit the latest paradox,
spit out all the sacrificed fingertips
in a cathartic form of self-expression,
all shotgun glittery and flophouse...

And everything just stared at you
in the wrong dosage,
in the wrong verses,
a fanatic sideshow cuddle,
peculiar and demolished,
advancing like a cheap makeup glacier,

Everything blurred faces,
everything metal and
sprained and out of season and
everything out of price range and
sticky and anyway,
I couldn't help but feel that this hypnosis
would seek to haunt itself tomorrow

because
injuries are impulsive,
because
the accidental gambit has won
on a molecular level,
because
on this late eventual afternoon
the convulsion of eruption identity
is acutely intoxicating like daisies...

Witness me —
because I am death and
because of death,
I'm definitely going to kick it up —
a festival of bombastic glory,
a bouncy habitual atrocity,
until someone closes the distance
with the correct decoding apparatus,
held like a gun between me
and my coward's genitalia,

The sweet homemade nectar of awakening...

A graphic and vacant crucifix threat
which could result in a pandemic of
pig-sticker divinity,
heaving operatically...

And in the big dumb aftershock,
I will stare into the fire and decide
it is only another sink to stick my head into,
but the autopilot declines me-
you can only bow so damn low...

Because a head can never hit the floor with
enough concussive force to break the disease,
unless it is deciphered by an executioner
with a flair for happy endings.

Lethe

The air is dead
unless you breathe it,

Exhaling a temple for each word
in the sound of its carved howling.

My heart is a crazy orbit,
a predatory star —
it will eat itself forever,
radiating language like celestial disaster,

And drink the intoxicating secrets
that would disappear into the lips of gods.

Gods who arrogantly insist
everyone must huddle,
remote in their shadows
which they drag about behind them
like sacks of wet grave dirt,
tracing meaningless glyphs onto the floor.

And if I am made in god's image
then god is my mirror,
my parlor trick -
a séance ghost carved out of water,
called forth into the room by my beckoning.

He says:
The fabric imitates the eternity of the corpse,
and I believe him.

As he crawls back behind the reflection,
a mad fluttering in the midst of his revelation
sounds strangely familiar,
like hearing your own voice underwater,

Provoking my own fixed mouth -
to make it murmur, to make it writhe,
to make it bubble a ring of crumbling stones,
grinding forth utterances
to form a conspicuous path until...

There is nothing left
but miles and miles of moving lips
plunging lost into the sea,
swimming in crippled halos,
difficult to comprehend,

As the delusional body of
my empty street
echoes with the eccentricities
of those crescent moons
succumbing to the void,

Where I dream deep within,
a madstone entombed
in the heart of a mountain,
and as my hands and feet
will bear witness,
there are no more wounds here.

Chanting towards the emptiness of
a pause, or some last intricate breath,

All my drowned words drift
just below the surface of the mirror,
revealing only flashes of
momentary illumination,

A reflection of the sun,
a kiss blown to my opposite,

The laughing death of a candle flicker
extinguished
by my own somniloquy.

Hoax

Primordial in afterthought,
the sacrificed animals heave hearts of
fertility and engineering, dreams and sentences,

Deconstructed to be adherents to
the infatuations of tension and constraint,
through which the relentless modulations of
witching clocks grind out their dread plots,

Forgetting that it is best to disregard
any temptation toward resemblance,
any willful attachment to faulty folklore,

And instead, endeavor to be blameless,
to take a wayward object and
fold it with care into a human-shaped charm,
placing within it a beating wing,
so that it may escape
any tempestuous insistence on definition.

For it would be much better to slake and stare
than to be obscured within an empty performance,
than to seek comfort where the
remnants of the beast still provoke shame,
the old symbols still legible and smoldering,
as meaningless as their initial annunciation
about what it meant to lie,

Or to be urged on by unknowing,
by a weeping armistice
concealing the forbidden forms
honed sharp into incriminating confessions,
deranged from thirsting for too long or
from stumbling vainly into the
quagmire deeds of the dead,

Resting assured in the promise of
a homecoming embrace,
an ironclad claim of ignorance,
to fade into sleep again in
the wasted perfume of yet another sacrifice,

Reaching
to where the sparks can only burn
to scatter so high,

And each
wink out
like a hoax,

One after another after another.

The Prescription for Burning (for Greg)

The afternoon is a determined, shadowy umber,
so burn it the rest of the way into a blackness
& declare it illuminated, if only by touch.

Onto a coarse cloth, lay down your conscience,
a benevolent measure,
assured & surrendered by the hand in
that obscure way of
holding onto the meaning, if only by a thread,
& redirecting it to spell out in a single glyph -
the devotion of budding aspiration.

What the hand puts down in casual stokes
the eye can only dream about confessing -
an absolute wounded tower
hidden in a spare green sprig,
ignited with red medicine.

Who would ask to be so illuminated,
just a kiss beyond the darkness?
The stain of single hewn captivation
versus a destructive way of saying,
a beholding in the incident,
intimidating like a prayer,

A prayer to know the color of a female form
so well
that she disappears into the past,
spoken in a syllable
so thin
it can only be streaked with memory,
so deep
that the intention is
slashed & declared complete
in a vague stroke of dusk-shimmered mercy,

And an oath that all the lit embers on
those tobacco colored nights wouldn't burn you,
as you vented negation with bare breath
back into the unseen sky,
knowing that the wind, it was not.

Cutting the night off, declaring the injured,
& asking to take a moment
just to smolder & hold to your inspiration,

Because breathing it all back out too willingly
would only inflict a wound so mortal
it would extinguish
your last declaration of conciliation.

Fingers Haunted by Dead Poets (for Lorca)

Phantoms always gather at
the carousel of drinking eyes
to keep watch as if moonlight or sunlight
will render impotent
the steady momentum of dominion absolutism,

While nearby
Mephistopheles hounds always gather,
lurking and waiting
with ears kept sharp
like blades temporarily bereft of blood,

And they will listen
for the sound of too much laughter,
and they will listen
so that the sea can continue
to leak its saline dream
into the mockery of battlefield mud,
with only the small mercy of
softening it up
for the jaws of the dead.

Another poet bound,
dragging words like wounds carved
into the faces of all the stopped clocks,
gut springs spilled and belly unwound,
gathered and burned
by a brutal and servile inferno,

A commandment of blind bullets
kissing shut
the defiance of all the lips,
stuffing silent
the defiance of all the throats.

And so many nights
I am a thirsty eye
wandering without sleep,
and fingers haunted by dead poets,
clawing at a too-heavy blanket of scribbles,
thinking beyond the sounds of rifles,
thinking beyond the stillness thereafter,
to the arriving illumination
against a propaganda that
marches counterclockwise to it.

Because your grave is my grave,
a secret still kept
by the shade of some unwilling tree,
because your voice is my voice,
hidden away by the undeserved,

Planted in like company
within the unleavened dirt,
that for the sake of the authentic
must be continually chewed
and then spat out
in a sad form of resurrection.

I, Ophelia

This cold month's body,
save my hand from turning too many door handles.
Stay bare here awhile, slack and still.

And these fecund hands look small now, like snow,
piled at the door of my little pieces of graves,

Bright songs around the edges scarred,
two poems that were left in the street
caught up in a gust,
and the prescribed debt of bleached ink
to the resolute sun.

In the door — naked female, skull matriarch,
the small sigh, song of my body.
I am a legacy of escape.

To speak is to sometimes go grey as the grave,
a riddle sought in the soil of bone dialects,
this idea of death, of my skull clean and
pecked at by worshipping birds,
then wreathed with violets.

See there? The reflection at the foot of the bed?
The floor all ready to receive our faultless sleep?

What ghost moves there,
displeased with its fine rookery?

The mirror skeleton tree,
shattering in a small dream,
to cut my feet.

It is a dream in colors and dark figures,
a ring of fire for all the sweet graves.

So sayeth the tomb back to the light,
and my cramped body, my silly head,
the dove, grey,
looking down the tip of the mouth,
dark with wrongful dust,
alighting on the tip of the worm.

I did not waste a woman's heart
for this legacy, did I?

I want to see the words grinning
around the mouth, the larynx,
the beloved skull kissed and entombed
in a silk curtain by knives,

And I say,
less and less brightly, too,
such as the sun can be obscured.

Poetry is not a sigh in the end of the mouth.
It slides through bone to hit the
reflection that rattles in the dark marrow,
the creeping hall of memory, and
this tree conceals a dread harpy,
watching for poetry in the carcasses,
a small sharp mouth, curiously hooked,
haunting the branches for months,
awaiting a sign.

Proof that death is that remedy prophesized
in the doorstops of mausoleums,
which are nothing more than flocks of doves
temporarily silenced of their mournful groaning,

Their thousands of beaks seeking,
and then choking on revenge.

Little Things I've Only Dreamt About

I have taken to heart everything,
but still the umbra is too unwilling
to watch a smile that occult
fade so swiftly
into a diminishing crescent.

And it is truly a cunning form
for your neck to turn
like my own moon does,
expectantly at the sound of
a door unlatching,
letting in just enough light
to lure a daring peek,

Where I hunger for and eat
all the fingers of your thin branches
setting free the hanging stars,

Letting them finally
stay up there on their own,
unbound and appeased,
drunk on the convenience of loft,

As your new armless botany
grows entangled
into my dreaming machine,
promising to block every window,

Only instead,
falling out of my head
like words about unadorned torsos,
leaving me to wonder if
I have deep enough fingers
to pick them all up,

Exquisite little things
that they are.

Antigone

Determined
to die,
by action of birthing
us
into the dark,

Who can hold their lips
closed in asylum?

Who creates the hands
that would allow their own rope
to go taut?

She,
who breaths upwards
only to keep the birds aloft,
to witness the city's
most arrogant architectures.

Sure will be her children.

Sure will be her children,
who hold no manufactured gods
in the agony of their solitude,

Sure will be her children,
who need no violence of apologies,

Sure will be her children
in their asphyxiated dreaming,

Held in breath,

Held in resolve,

Held in a loop of boundary
eternally tied,

Tired but unyielding,

Like the weeping
eye of a noose.

Anteros

It was good luck for the first time,
the first line at miserable.
You, in kindled disruption,
glittered with disappearances,

Walking through the charms
in a shortage of blooms,
at risk,
without so much as a shiver,

Invoking the communion on
consummate legs,
a delving indulgence,
abstracted in waves of trance allure.

I will hold you for a while,
I will carry you on a fevered shell,
I am afraid that I am strange
and that I will not bore you
with my fingers,

Devoutly intent on finding a means
to go haunting your tenderest of burials.

The greatest thing I did was
to provoke the impunity of clouds
into a leavening,

To believe all day that
remaining hallowed to the peculiar
was a way to wake the divine,
if only to satisfy your native shapes
and articulations.

Like the deceased who
believed that they were dead,
yet were impatient
in their disappearances,
unbridled,

I gathered up
their mistrust in shadows and
sought out the sunlight,
craving the clarity of your prediction.

I do not know why.
I just wanted one last step forward,

My wishes, spare and undefined,
doused in abdomen and hip bone furor,
pushing at the afflicted breach.

Do not panic at this touch.
Do not leave it all in my hands -

I am going to carve you into
a brief message,
one that will fill a landscape with hunger.

You see,
you are the first diversion
from contradictions
I have seen, and

I am a coward,
tentatively seeking to become a
compliant hostage of
your milk and honey empire.

When the Morrígan Asked to Be My Muse

I am calling out to you,
a group of small characters
filling the intersection with withering.

Fear, that genius, is the best poet by nature,
and loves to dissolve satisfaction into
the most wordy diversions
and distorted language emblems,
a handful of writhing larva to figure out.

Some singing dreamer asked me
to place a small wager on
a group of phantoms who cried at my door
when the letter was doubted,
because they seemed strange in other towns
because of me,
because I also cried nearby,
like floral contemplation,
head heavy with drizzle and
gnawed by pests.

I delicately rolled the moon over
and buried myself in its underbelly,

Concealing myself within this new cell —
a four walled concoction of
polymorphic ghosts and falling feathers,
my doubt, always near,
perched on my neck,
and the door always threatening its
substitute flesh.

Ill luck was paid out as my reward,
wings unfolding,
strange and speechless and not at all funny,
but I'm laughing anyway, because

These absurd dark birds are certainly small,

But when they crush,
they never say a word about suffocation.

Mephistopheles is Ready for His Portrait Now

There is an irritating beauty in weariness,
something you and I could get accustomed to,
if you would just deconstruct your hairstyle,
& if I could somehow crop all the pulp blood
out of the scene.

But someone's got all these so-called good guys
out there beating the streets to death
with blunt-force assumptions,
leaving the irresolute so lonely
they're prowling in their own halls
looking for punishment,
hammering on their mirrors until
their reflections look like they shouldn't,
like corrupted admonitions in the funhouse.

Where some weirdo you never heard of is
shouting at you to let the curtain drop,
but I'm trying to tell you
that there is no goddamned curtain,
unless you count on alleged reputations.

So go on, break open all those seals.
I'm fucking ready.

Bleed me into your dirt & and the fruit
will be all the more plentiful.

Because there are no people
like reflectionless people,
mere replications of their Judas kisses,
& it's like I tried to warn you —
most of the time they're just
praying into their own portraits,
looking for a compelling escape clause,
their bodies ripe with unrequited requests,

Which I shrewdly stage and rearrange until
they see me in their deepest suspicions & confessions,
the growing shadow of a pagan savior looming
ravishingly against the gates of their consecrated city,

Asking them to make sure and smile for the camera.

Sing Us a Song so That so Many Poets Will No Longer Need to Commit Suicide

I.

I could be red cruelty,
the wound which refuses to heal,
a mouth
that stitches conversations into silence.

I am bound mad within the wound,
because to cease is
to exist within the abundance of death
asleep in the meaning.

One face to live, to write from,

One face to drink from Lethe.

What fear? What hush?
What sound? What dream?

I hide in my own marrow,
in the marrow of these marginal proposals,
which are my own entanglement,
my sustenance and ruse.

Devised in a violation of self,
crowning
despite all their discomforts.

Damned to writhe in linguistic mirages,
to choke in grand atmospheres,
to respire through
the accumulation of drowning impediments.

Seeking shelter within labyrinthine architecture,
only to deconstruct it in blind excavation,
to cancel out the rigor mortis of shape.

An emotion is called black because of the color,
but what of the color of crows?
Do they receive such scrutiny
because of what they appear to be on the outside?
Little dabs of metaphor in a green field,
merely seeking to endure loss and interrogation?

No one can cut cleaner edges,
given only blunt scissors for wings.

Transformation of words into savage machines,
connected by corridors that conduct
the blood of the dead,
the language and power of the dead,
the fearlessness contained
in their paralyzed tongues.

Distillation of brilliance and lunacy,
a duplicity of madness carved out in opaque sigils,
eroding inert language by law of silence.

Nothing brushes the sky
like a perfectly written black bird,
splashed in spreading ink,
complete in divine velocity,
its wilderness voice
beyond the abstract barriers of
inarticulate hesitation.

I opened a breach in the twilight with my sun,
my eye full of blind love that
seeks every color
reflected from both sides of the restless flutter.

A burdened mechanical existence,
built to dissect implications
presumed to be smoldering in the voluminous cracks
between every letter and word on the already
decaying pages.

My silence is a myth of two heads,
it is a changeling state of degeneration,
the loss of cohesive language,
born in the afterbirth and ashes of the hunt.

So I must apologize — it was very cruel of me
to disguise myself as a poem.

As punishment,
let me go blind from the allure,
the eyes,
drinking up fountains of bitterness and implication
in order to redefine my focus as embodiment.

Collect this blood, my own Asperges,
cast it and hold it accountable
for the strange feathering designs
it makes on the floor
in attempted explanation,
before it trickles away to the gutters.

A reasonable solution
to quell a large breach in a fading beast,
eternally perched within my hands,
waiting to cannibalize its next rejuvenated heart.

And having been born
during the hour of the bell's loudest chiming,
it is as I have always
suspected —

I am the horizon
that Death seeks,
in vehement strides throughout the sky,

Measured out
one pretty little sentence
at a time.

II.

Sing us a song
so that so many poets
will no longer need
to commit suicide,

So that the finishing stone
will not create
a precipice in the heart
from which to leap.

Lest another mound of soil
and crumbling disguise of flesh
become enshrouded by a frail snail shell,
rattling out its own
hollow song of insolvency.

I praise each bird,
broken from flight's toils,
ask each to become a luminosity,
to alight in the spontaneous sky,
until the last star's glimmer
is replaced by the thunder
of their beating wings.

Their inevitable beaks cracking
the interstellar boundary.

She asked me to find the noise of her feet
while sailing on a boat through warm blood,
but the wild waters had already
been amputated into wakes and eddies
by a wooden tongue asking questions.

Reciting a flawed perception of
splintering shorelines,
reflected in the imitation of light
at the end of a long spiraling sentence.

An eroded copper cliff,
deliberately muttering a ring
of feet composition in wet sand -
all that remains of the ceremony.

And there,
I dreamt I was the man
carving driftwood effigies
out of the grey faces of strangers.

I wore an entire city
around my neck,
a small bird followed me
like a chime,
confused by the sound of its own
curious pecking.

But even the sounds of
hallowed birds must pass -
just as echoes lose their color timidly,
just as chains hold their grip fast
in their own suppressing sound,
until the coda of rust
is exhaled at last.

While I parcel up my isolation,
others make the sounds of flesh
with their mouths,
emulating the voices of their fixations,
reciting tarnish into their crumbling mirrors,
screaming at the audience to pay attention.

I never acquired a taste for such noise
during my noctivagant wandering
among the vacant and hungry stars,
anonymous patterns obscured in the dim,
sweeping within one another,
discovering that language is just
a gathering of birds sent soaring
after the world's vast extravagance,

Only to die of elegant starvation
while on the wing,
falling into the prone shape of a man.

A specific kind of gravity
that can only be understood
though the feat of pulsing wings,
and a prescience that the birds
will never stop migrating their blue pages
just to fall into the trap of arrangement.

I have been repeatedly
spat out of that sky,
and justly so,
fluttering in a stirring of occasional winds,
descending in a vague, tapering tone of absence,

Left to fool,

A human shaped echo
of what should have been
a beautiful mirage.

III.

If you are capable
of speaking with your own voice,
whisper only in ashes
so that the takers of flesh
will not notice
and bloom their flowers
in your throat.

The death of the body
is stillness,
the shortage of a word is muted
by fear of sleeping in parting ground.

Purgatory soot dusted fingers
scrawling with burnt ends of bones,
lighting tongues for incense,
each fountainhead of aromatic smoke
cocooned in a shrine of sediment,
dreading the work of permeation
like some profane violation of holy ground.

Death alights on desperate hands
with the promise of transmutation,
offering an inscription to the cosmos
from the storm within the body,
the prolonged night hidden in the volatility
of too much heart to disguise.

Somehow, I lost your bird within me,
my face sinking in shame like a half-moon
paled beneath the dark water,
scribbling a note in the middle of a road:
If you read the sea, remember…

I hide in my little notes,
embodiments of the embers from
some strangely familiar figure,
winding through the black,
a smoke snake,
trailing a convincing dusk
through a halo of stars,
restlessly pacing
the dark ramparts of an elegy.

Birds writing their nests of words
did not beg for their fear of mortality
to be inflicted by indifferent teeth.

To live and to eat these minor terrors
is to build them up
in front of your own reflections.

Gather up these moments
and throw away the handouts –

Death sent me a mirror.

And I spent the sea there,
in the substantial body of a female,
sheltered in the mirror's black
to stop the reflectionless joy
of my only word: unknowing.

And,
as before,
I died alone,
frozen in the heart
of a crow's silent fall.

IV.

When you were a child,
what calling birds did you try to fall asleep to?
Hiding from the hell of tangled blankets,
weeping beneath the night's conspiracies,
breathing through too many open windows?

Did you wince
from the height of you own voice,
hearing the sound of its yearning
from below?

Stuttering on the potable words
you drank from,
words that would one day
become a storm that would submerge
your lost days.

The secreted notes from
anagogic grave robbers
delivered to your dreaming forehead
in beads of sweat
like a lost address,

Exponentially expanding drag
to ultimately overcome
any lift you gained
from carefully unfolding all the voices.

Admired for your
melancholy instrument,
tuned and forgotten,
but not lost,
from a childhood begged forth
in the delicate mechanism of the wrist,

And singing out of blind doll eyes
to an inversion of images,
seeking the elusive fortunes
divined from the ashes of feathers and bones.

In the end, it was the way it had to be,
your words were mirrors of your footsteps,
a bridge of little works,
little flower drifts, little fugues.
An oeuvre scrawled in defiance
with a punctuation of barbiturates,
choosing to let your words fall asleep
on another indifferent Monday.

V.

Within this seeking
there are only endless spirals
spilling out of a melancholy ocean,

And the grey countryside painted
in a melody of crow's dust and soot,

Forever reminding that
loss can be a virtue,
real as rain and
easy as drowning.

In a bare cast room,
listening to Polyhymnia embodiments
insert black commas
as waypoints to reflection.

Opening all of the books,
with their covers of dead brittle faces,
forcing a breach between
each jaw to locate the fluttering signs
in the breath.

Rime eventually settled on me
through the gaps in the stars
painted on my face,
and I shivered.

Nocturnal,
we all live by the grim grey stones
we are born from,
and continue to carve them away to pebbles.

So what color face now,
my poor dead crow?
To whom shall I pass you,
down into the stillness?

Where all the oceans are female,
their waves painted over with ghost paper,
their eyes,
trembling moth wings.
Passing the time by twisting
fragrant poem poppets
out of dried flowers and sticks,
to inflict dreams of hunger
upon lonely vigils.

All the remains are gathered,
rearranged and deciphered
in no particular order,
into the waning colors of twilight -

A joke, because everyone knows
the true color of a poem is in its
wayward sparks.

And in reading them,
I will pass you,
mortally wounded and
abandoned deeply,

Sitting in a dead tree,
casting a somewhat dimmer shadow —
but a shadow still —

Across my upturned face.

Harmonia in Absentia

Image is a fake skin, an aftertaste,
an external stimulus imitating the wings in
the vocal cords, coughing a sense of imbalance,
the belief that you are awake and
I am substantial and we are cheap to die in
the doubting of indiscriminate riddles
placed the way heaven can never be accompanied
down a stolen drain.

An additional day of love must mean
that you are being deceived somehow,
like the melodious sound of sex leaves gouges of
vivid phantoms and corporeal ejecta
in the peeling off of zippered apprehension,

Senses tangled within the bestial fruits and
you thought you were just going to be
an involuntary place of worship,
disguised as a slip of the tongue,
a patsy always seeking out injury.

Excuse me, is this the illusory department?
My mistake.

All these raw days are actually just
my shoes mixed up with the hip bones,
my bodily excerpts interlaced within
the evacuating light and how typical –
a sham hypothesis emulated in the creeping of
an apparatus and not so generic in its dream of
being wretched, to the point where I am leaking and
also this might be goodbye, AKA I love you,
and we should probably make for the applause soon
because to wake up is a lonely process and
anyway I really think that we are dissolving.

And it's ending, it's definitely ending.
I mean, can't you feel the curtains closing in?

Can't you hear the melancholy grinding of
a million, billion bed springs?

Binary Collapse

Specious discourse
from a flirtatious sky,

It was such an
untimely rest
for an approximate body.

Say the way,

Yes, that leaves you
thinking in
zero gravity and tumbling,
interface and decline,

And the visible spectrum too,
where I wait for your approach,
despite my heresy of
blind longing.

Say the way,

Yes, these bodies will falter,
and no one can be divine
in the place where
I want to end my lunge.

Say the way,

To reveal an ordained tear,
a place to bite our fiery tongues
into begging,
for a dividing of your heavens
into slow slicing of eclipse,

Until it is far too late
to throw knots into this
ravenous embrace of
our inevitable circumvolutions.

Symbiotic Monsters

To remain
cautiously equipped
is no evidence of ferocity,
and monuments to assemblage
are always available for rental.

Learn more, learn less,
about inescapable adornment,
about stealing in gestures,
I do not care —
there is no glory without complicity.

I will go again,
to be present within just one person,
a steady pull from hesitation -
you learn about direction by
going the other way.

Do you emit black,
or do you just lurk there,
impersonating the corner?

I certainly appreciate
your funeral, your monstrosity,
your synthesis of poison into a

tangible evaluation, and
I regretted like I believed —
my intercourse was devout,

One sabotaged mouth
breathing tremors into another.

Illusionary, burning heavy,
subtle sounds of silted eye and saliva,
the body's door pierced
by sacrificial slivers, a slight,
suffocating etiquette,
tilting at the sky
due to an error in refraction,

Misunderstanding
in the midst of an autopsy,
insisting that its meaning be
manifested in wanton insertions,
in worms, in leeches,
in violations and

A key is just a key,

A hope for turning the body open
like a chaotic jaw, determined,
gnawing an interference gape,
to dredge what is rousing
beneath monotone sighs,

My upright infinity,
accustomed to copulations with ghosts,
desires touched off by
decomposing your opaque phrases
about too many limbs,
too many arms to remain in these
insufficient shapes
that at times will mimic spiders.

Just like ordinary flowers tell us —
imitation of form is hallucination.

So good luck with your foray,
you and your weepy, weepy eyes.

Beating Down Words Like Nails

The word I created is lost
or maybe just abandoned
as a likeness of living.

Cut thin in just places,
a deep body of grey salt,
endless and worn thirsty.

A bunch of brittle books
about a fair share of sin &
fumbling remuneration.

The charade body
gathered & dragged,
wilted & lost to falling,
in the constant pace of
pinwheels.

Smoke as you peer homewards.

Depleted prestige
& the endless waning,
a place without all this eternal weight,
& I'm just putting down sediment.

Within this monolithic tangle,
your body's poetry wilts
upon speaking,

Connected by this hand
to a portion of milky thoughts
& digging fingers into faintness.

This business will be finished.

I am famine & this toil is weightless.
Your body is a hunger.

Mine is just lost
like some crazy idea, like a
half-hearted attempt at connection.

Shipwrecks

Revenant in words and ideas,
a reverse optical trickster that
picks people up and broadcasts
their proclamations
into the interstellar maelstrom,

While former constellations
wept during scrutiny,
Argo Navis was split into three,
and sank into the deep, dark sea,

Away from the light of the monitor,
praying for a silt of comforting restraint,
or a pretty and dangerous tracking error
in the stratigraphic column,

A warbling from within that
moved against the universal spin,
a self-imposed ceiling
and a quiet place to drown,
improbable and schismatic.

There are many sad ways to live —
making it impossible to judge
intergalactic distances from
beneath a slight hesitation in
surface tension,

The way some photons seem to
always find their way back down
into muddy puddles,

While others insist on travelling to
a thousand different places
they'll never actually get to.

Siege Engine

I am in love with my own anathema
and its small deaths are only temporarily crushes.

Flowing now, empty later,

All blockades are confessed into the world,
like a trembling face,
held captive as yesterday's picked bellflower,

Hiding in a gap between two effigies
like some ghostly impression,
stitched into an incursion by phrases,
insinuating a piercing of nervous perimeters,

A passionately locked window and
my eagerly awaited imprisonment,
where purpose is broken down
into its component lessons about willpower,

Where an honest collapse is jealous
of the melancholy trap of commitment,
the shivering, starving foundations
wrenching against their obstacles,
if only to get to the other side of the room,

Where I can barely stand to breathe
for want of this foolish violation of structure,

In too deep and rightly embarrassed
that I even asked the question,
brimming with desperation and
drowning in your pretty poison.

Psalm

The prayer of you has been sanctified,
a change in the ratio of inarticulate patterns,
an eloquent broadcast of turbulence into
the perception of mirages.

All magic, but no electricity, from this body dust.

And the knowledge that the separation of
skin into fictitious walls and slowly diving elegies
will only leave a craving for the wet allure of
a contraband euphoria.

Only you embody the quality of loosened knots,
dreaming about the number of birds nests
you hope to untangle and reassemble into paucity.

Only you will exhale a clear breath
into the shudder of another night's empty redemption,
working out the value of some underwhelming memory.
Left alone to swallow your own temperament,
fit only for a dancing flame.

We are all willing hostages
peering from behind paper walls,
hidden and gnashing and waiting for decay,

waiting for these bitter days to end,
turning grey in the looming indifference of the sun,
until distance finally teaches us its invaluable lesson,

When the empty spaces will have to fear falling into us.

Nice to Meet You

I may have been exhausted
but my wounds were acting
strangely until now,
and I am still walking home,

And because I expected myself,
I lurked around every corner —
none were found without me so far,
and I've certainly been around
to all the ordinary institutions with
their flawed obsessions with sustentation.

But I will appear only when
the right weather is difficult to come by,
when three sparked birds
keep a dream of waking in the eyes
and I am holding very still,
beyond the light of the misleading door.

Appearing first
as a bruised man doing nothing,
and then later,
wanting to burn whatever I wanted,
but I wanted to be with you
because I always knew
we were nothing but lingerers
waiting to ignite one another.

Nice to meet you, you said,
breathing in the ashes of our union.

Nice to meet you, I said,
with flecks of your lost
and indecipherable caress
burning pinholes
in my darkest of jackets.

Pirouette

There is a request that fades me like a ghost -
I asked for an exit, but I was nervous about circles.

Winding together, we should turn around and go,
to try and escape by clever bending and breathing,

Not begging for a fracture of splintering edges,
only the dexterity of verses, lithe within each gasp,

Until the passages are overgrown with brambles &
like a rumination, the moon will not be swayed.

Such a vulnerability does not matter
to the one who broke it down into phrases,

Or the one who understands its unraveling flaw & how
in the end, it will once again pirouette into oblivion,

Where we too are sent, to go on splitting into breaths,
until there is a last fade in the light, and no more favors,

An overabundance of descent with each advance,
so that we no longer need to worry about our pace,

Because we know we will break this bread a thousand times
over & each time, the curves will grow sharper and tighter,

Like the last ringing that escapes a tolling bell,
like a reassurance of birds, searching for a place to land.

Achlys' Lips, Wet With Mercy

She plucked a shiver off of the leaf and
wrapped her misty shawl around the sleeper,
with a grace that I would end up begging for,
as small as my minutes would wantonly allow.

Distant and enchanting like asylum,
a sooty and terse candle
with a demanding shimmer
like the business ends of spears,
eager to hew the skin into a creviced pact,
to introduce little wanton admissions and
shudderings, grinding up whispers,

Sharpening the delicate wounds,
cutting them more breathless than miserable,
a looting of sinew and inflamed blood that
would never be absolved of risk.

And if I could, I might coax a bend
in the remoteness of her knees, her thighs,
provoking them into a spiraling staircase,
the flexion unfolding into a stumble of
temporary eyelids, a flutter,
a subtle appreciation for tremors
induced by a beading of tears,
wept from her undeniable vertex,

The lascivious stage where a
forbidden passage spawned within me
the falseness of a pierced dialect,
and adoringly, I pledged:

I will heave thy thatch into tangles.

I will bless thy niche still,
murmured by my lips in worship.

Drinking in the sacred violations until
ruthlessly intoxicated and spent,
entranced enough to stare up at the stars
and see only a philosophy of traps,
slinking faintly through the falling ashes
tithed within her scant cathedral walls,

Where she spelled out revelation with
a sentence of gravestone assurances,
not even thinking that it might serve
to ensnare me —
one end wrapped around
the assumption of my neck,
the other fastened around penance,
caught in the narrowing space between
a pendulum of subdued flesh and
a beguiling gate ringed with harrow,

Her lips, wet with mercy,
wet with ease, wet with certitude,
the elegance of a precarious imprint of
a body bruised onto fresh blossoms,
spreading with the suggestion of a kiss,

And everything else, a bitter cast breath,
raising a compensation of horripilation
onto the expanse of my barren,
parchment-like soul.

Minotauros

I am waiting with patience
for the ground's color to creep into me,
bending into the mirror of the maze,

To be abandoned,
to be hounded
by the sounds such words can capture,

Faulty behind the mask of a beast.

I am bleak,
depicted by the shadows of
my own boundary —
it is hard to hate something
you yourself took such great care
to corrupt,

Your chalk and blood brooding,
a false structure aligned
with a choking that cuts the rocks
into a reoccurrence of scrawls —
the same old story and foil.

Unbroken and unrealistic,
but also heartsick and desirous,

a dark that laps at the light,
attentive like a curse,

As a fertile flaw
conceiving itself,

Winding and winding,
the maze arises in you
and you will tear it apart
with taurine brashness
forever,

To scatter the pieces behind,
in a form of hindsight,
an inability to be abandoned
ever again.

Your hunger — struggling to wait,
this is the gorge of you,
this is the emptiness
that will satisfy
only in an apology of bones,

Deep in your absolute monstrosity.

The Colossus Has Always Been Hollow

The name was made only to allure,
and I was a word waiting in my quiet fingers.
The tension was a dream,
inhaled and drained out of the eyes
like two strangers.

I moved my body through the air,
a row of irregularities without a proposal,
desperate to manipulate perspective,
like spilling mercury out of a glass.

And I craved the air in the corner,
lumbered toward it like a Trojan Horse,
because the word must always be entered,
a quick arousal like a tiny death,
hidden in a basket of paper birds,

And the one you pluck out to set free
will be the one that consumes you
as if you were a worm.

Maybe you have heard of my promise,
one of the loneliest I have ever talked about —
I hoped to be a succession of chapters
but instead ended up a dusty library,
where no one ever came to read.

Kiss me there, in my room of silence,
a room buried deep in a signal,
like a hanging breath,
like a cessation of hostilities,
devoted to finding the stopper in a nimbus,
to release the final flood.

How I longed for the watery miracle,
but the moon, refusing its shape,
dropped seductively behind the clouds,
any remaining light spilling out in omens,
contorting into varying degrees of concealment,

Refusing to anoint my eyes with its language,
hidden in the guise of an unconnected hand,
an empty starfish, or maybe a falling glove,
a prediction of my nature,
bereft of any means to grasp,

Leaving me to hang on
the only way I know how.

Daughter of Nix

I want to be a whisper to you,
in the shape of you and the sound of
a devoted tongue in the hills,
a salt figure abandoned to
your movements of darkness.

I want to be a voyeur
of the voices in your void,
where inwardness is cloudy and
I have bloomed, beloved as burst thunder.

Loitering in the middle of the body
paging through a book
about doomsday and Ouija boards,

My mouth notching an arrow
into your ambush.
Begging that you lie down and
be affixed to this burning arc,

Drawn to the stroke
in my throwaway intrusion.

Liminal Deities

While my eyes may be
on the verge of starvation
my hands are a proven sin,
beautifully carved
into amulets and good luck charms,

And where I am gracefully fractured,
I am pleased with my pain —
how it accurately traces
all the way back to the intersection of
each inception until just out of sight,
as if I will somehow finally
learn how to disappear.

It can't be a coincidence that
I have an occupied face
but an empty stare.
Normally I am guilty of the
ferocious crime of becoming wayward,
but my concern for being debunked
compels me to avoid crossing paths
with the throat traffickers
and all their suffocating small talk
about how the neck
can be a tenuous transit.

Instead, I point out
the impracticality of the heart
and cross it,
as if it were some fearless calamity,
as if it were some defector,
as if it were some sort of
casualty of accountability.

Standing at the threshold
between the hallway and the door,
I am going to step out
onto the floor of my charade
and pray that it doesn't creak too loudly,
attracting the attention of other,
even more fictitious methods of egress,

And should an antagonist
happen to be within earshot,
I strongly suggest a diversion —
a vivisection of your own mortality,
with the understanding that
my divine covenant prevents me
from redefining any of your wounds,

For the ground is a dread place
to spill your entire allotment,
too parting, too occasional and too eager.

But when you are accumulated again
comfortably in the tongue,
I will promise to rebuke
all your remaining misalignments,
so you can finally have
a long and peaceful night's sleep,

The kind of sleep that wears like a talisman,
warding off any attempts to impede
the odyssey of dreaming.

Jim McGowin does art but keeps a day job. He has been published in Chance Operations, The UCity Review, Rusty Truck, The Gasconade Review and has authored several chapbooks. He lives in St. Louis, MO with his family and two cats.

This project was made possible, in part, by generous support from the Osage Arts Community.

Osage Arts Community provides temporary time, space and support for the creation of new artistic works in a retreat format, serving creative people of all kinds — visual artists, composers, poets, fiction and nonfiction writers. Located on a 152-acre farm in an isolated rural mountainside setting in Central Missouri and bordered by ¾ of a mile of the Gasconade River, OAC provides residencies to those working alone, as well as welcoming collaborative teams, offering living space and workspace in a country environment to emerging and mid-career artists. For more information, visit us at www.osageac.org

www.ingramcontent.com/pod-product-compliance
Lightning Source LLC
Chambersburg PA
CBHW021447080526
44588CB00009B/729